# the most beautiful woman in shanghai

## scott shaw

**Buddha Rose Publications**

The Most Beautiful Woman in Shanghai
Copyright © 1987 By Scott Shaw
www.scottshaw.com
All Rights Reserved

No part of this book may be reproduced in any manner without the expressed written permission of the author or the publishing company.

First Edition 1988
Second Edition 2014

ISBN: 1-877792-24-1
ISBN 13: 978-1-877792-24-3

Library of Congress
Control Number:2014936948

10 9 8 7 6 5 4 3 2 1
Printed in the United States of America

*for wen ping*

*The Most Beautiful Woman in Shanghai*

1.

I have won
once or twice
but all I got was second best
but today
I was given
the most beautiful girl
on the airplane
and I have won it all

she is chinese
she is stunning
and she would not
even understand
what I said

she is tall thin
a good girl
if you know what I mean

of all that has been won
and all that has been lost
nothing even comes close
to the meeting of her
the most beautiful girl on the airplane

2.

the chains of passion
could I be playing for keeps
the bounds of love
and the boundaries thereof
what can I do
now that I have found you
all the years I have planned
how I would react
but what can I do
now that I have seen you
is it the road
to no more illusion
in a dreamer's mind
you are so perfect
so asian
so pure
everything that I have dreamed of
but now
that the dish is placed
within my hands reach
I do not know what to do

a dreamer with nothing to offer
a lust crazed artist
looking for the next player

can the playing ever stop
I do not know
it is all so confusing
at one time in my life
I would have given everything
to know you
but now that I have met you

I do not even wish to touch you
I do not want to tarnish you

but can I just walk away
because I know that if I touch you
I could not go away
never go away and forget
forget
like a player is forgotten
kissed hello/kissed goodbye
nothing gained
but you
you are the everything
and it does scare me

3.

her chinese skin touches mine
and
first touch/best touch
I am in love with her
we dance
so slowly
cheek-to-cheek
my arms around her
hers around me
close
as it will never be again
      for the first touch
      is the only touch
      as her chinese skin touches mine

4.

come here
my L.A. lady
come here
and hug me goodbye
for I have found myself
a new love
a lady of shanghai

she is so beautiful
oh so beautiful
she has all the style
that you have
and in shanghai
that is hard to come by

love
oh yes
there is no doubt
so come here
my L.A. lady
come here
and hug me goodbye

5.

a ticket out
I have never thought of myself
that way
maybe a ticket in
maybe even a ticket around
but out?
it all seems so calculated

now, I have taken
one or two for a ride
of this I cannot lie
and I have paid our way(s)
up and about
so I have paid my dues
now I have come close
once or twice
but never
close enough to know

but is this
this the time

ticket out
way out
I have been told
I am hers
what a way to see it
does she see it that way

6.

I write
I love you in chinese
for I love you
in chinese

chinese town
closed for so long
shanghai
once an open city
once
a long time ago
forty years later
and here we are
the 1980's
nearing the end of the 1980's
and here I am
here in shanghai
in shanghai
in love with you

where else could it be
where else could it be more perfect than
in shanghai
in the late 1980's
in love with you
so I write it
I write I love you
I write it in chinese

7.

I wait for my loves arrival
waiting…
something I never do
but today
I sit

she is fashionably late
fashionably
and in shanghai

oh yes
she does have fashion
oh yes
she does have style
and if I never wait for her again
today
I sit here
and write of her glories
so many so
that I wait
until now

she is here

8.

I feel old
I am here holding
and loving
to the maximum
this twenty-four year old
chinese maiden
and I stop
to write these words

she is loving me
and giving me
her first kisses
and I write
I feel old

9.

the nights of shanghai
I ride through the streets
in a taxi
the tape machine
is playing
soft pop
chinese music
on my shoulder
lie sleeping
a lady of love
a lady
who is filling my heart
and my lips
with her first kisses
I stare off into the city streets
chinese neon
in the windows
it glows
the buildings rise
    old and weather beaten
I ride through
the nights of shanghai

this could be heaven
I wonder why
I am not having a peak experience
for all my dreams
lay on my shoulder
    sleeping softly
as the music plays
and as the night goes by

10.

it will never be
this day again
a perfect day
in its own way
and I rode through it
so mild mannered
so removed
covered by the sheets
of drastic illusion
with a love
who continually slept
on my shoulder

today
was the first day
that I held her hand
today
was the first day
that I told her
that I loved her
today
was the first day
that she told me that she loved me
and today
was the first day
that our lips met
     and it will never be
     this day again

I hold her in my arms
and I wonder
can I ever stop

being the player
that I am

I hold her
for she is all
I have ever dreamed of
        style in shanghai
        not an easy thing to come by
and if I were to let her slip away
it would forever be my loss

yes, I hold her
yes, I love her
and today
it will never come again

11.

how can I tell her
that I am not what she thinks I am
how can I explain
that I am a dreamer
lost in a world
with no more dreams

she will want me
to buy her the moon
of which
she is a worthy exchange

but a businessman
I am not

so I smash my head
against the wall

me, I am a mystic
but how can I tell her
but how can I explain
for I know
she will want it all
all of which she deserves
but my all
and her desired all
are obviously
two very different things

how can I tell her
how can I explain

12.

can it be true
that the illusion dies so fast
so fast
too fast for me
can it be
that by seeing through the facade
illusion is broken
broken into little bits
little bits of nothingness

all I can say
is all I know
for sure
and that is
I sit here
awaiting my loves return
having seen the truth
having seen through the lies
and all I can do
is be sad
for the illusion
was so quickly shattered

13.

it is raining outside
on this china day
it is raining
and you know
I love the rain
awh, to walk in it
to spin in it
to play in it
and the wetter the better
but will my china doll
will she love it too
can she be
as free as me
perhaps, I may never know

14.

I think that I am broken hearted
that is the only thing
that could explain
the way I feel
I think that my heart is broken
not from her not loving me
but from me
not loving her

she is everything
and wants to be more
I am nothing
and prefer it that way
she longs to forever
lay in my arms
but I
the player that I am
can never give her that
so I sit here
and I cry a tear or two
I cry for the perfect love
which I have found
the perfect love
I have found
and cannot have

I think that my heart is broken
that is the only thing
that can explain
the way I feel

15.

hours spent
in a hotel room
reminiscent
of other times
other countries/other women
holding
loving
cannot get enough
well maybe...
and is this the only reason
I have traveled so far
    the promise of
    the promise for
and tomorrow
will it never come
so I guess all I want
is one more kiss
one more kiss goodbye

as the illusion fades
into reality
and the truth of the reality
takes hold

so slam my head
against the wall
bang it
one more time

everything
it becomes nothing
when everything is had
and nothing remains

so kiss me
one more time
tell me
you will give me
all I need

and I will dream about it forever
but forever
is so close at hand

hours of time
in the hotel room
it fades into the gray
the gray of the rainy shanghai sky

and it will be
as it never was
it will be
as it already is
and I
I will go away

16.

I take my shanghai love
to a french restaurant
a french restaurant
in china
I take her
and watch
as she tries to eat
european style
I teach her
a thing or two
awh, what an elegant lady
      an elegant lady
      waiting to be born
but she has been locked
inside the walls
of the people's republic
never seeing the light of day

yes, I could break her out
but the price
it is oh so high
…though I may pay it
for I have paid prices
asked before
but I need to know
if she is true
or simply another illusion
of the world

so the bill
it came to around
about $160.00 u.s.

and
as I would do for her
I simply signed the paper
and put it
on my platinum credit card

17.

I wish I could remember
more clearly
the first time
that I caught her glance
but that moment
has been washed
into the hours of melancholy
thrown into the funeral pyre
of time
but in my vague memory
of a moment
not long ago gone by
I know that I would have agreed with her
that she is
as she claims
the most beautiful woman
in shanghai

there are not many features
of her face
that stand out
none that may be described
but perhaps
in that simplicity
is where her beauty truly lies

in a country
lost in its own masses
few have an image
to call there own

but if style
were a visual prison
than she may be the lost guard
and than
I must agree with her
that she is
the most beautiful woman
in shanghai

I wish when we said goodbye
that there could have been
more romance
but in a world
just now catching up with time
passion
is a farmer's joy
and a city man's dream

I suppose that I could not argue
that she does have her faults
but if
push came to shove
tooth came to nail
I would have to agree with her
that she is
the most beautiful woman
in shanghai

when I finally left her
I knew I could only dream of my return
and when I drove away
I knew I had seen

my last chance
at loving virtue

but when a player is
as a player does
there can only be the game
so all I could do
was walk away and dream

as I look back on our last kiss
I cannot even remember
when it was
but I would have to agree with her that
it was given to me
by the most beautiful woman
in shanghai

18.

she told me
when she saw me she knew
I was for her
well, I have to admit
had I been asked the question
my answer
would have been the same
but I cannot remove
the idea/the thought
from my mind
that all this is not
as it seems
I cannot erase the idea
that somewhere/someone
is playing the game

she holds me
she loves me
gives me her first kiss
but first kiss/last kiss
can it be true
how can I ever know

19.

*when I saw you*
*I knew*
so the words
came out of her mouth
when I saw her
all I could do was wish
but isn't that the dance
related down through the ages
isn' that always
the pagan words spoken
for only one is allowed to know
one allowed to wish
in any game
the winner is
the one who makes up the rules
and now that she knows
does she really know
who and what I really am
no, I do not believe so
for how could she
in a society
where there is no such thing
as a lost and wandering poet
no such thing as a mystic dreamer
lost in the night

so,she knows
I am the one
me, I know nothing
I am left out here
deep out here
in the lost
chinese extremities

wondering
exactly what are
the rules of the game

20.

I guess
I wish
I would have found her in tokyo
where there is more freedom
in the air
where we could walk the streets
*hand-in-hand*
and have coffee
in the cafes at night

I guess
I wish
we had more time
to do nothing
with no one looking on

and I guess
I wish
I loved her more
for than nothing else
would even matter

21.

every tear I cry
will forever
be cried for you
because I will never
see you again
every tear I cry
will forever
be cried for you
because it was you
who I had dreamed of
my entire life
but the world
and its lies
      its lies
      its governments
      its politics
they all keep us apart
every tear I cry
will forever
be cried for you
and with your every thought of me
another tear I will cry

22.

arising feelings
of worthless love
love
that is trapped
in its appropriate box
love
that is lost in a culture
that will not let it go

I sit
in beijing
I sit
in the late evening
I sit
all alone
and I wish
that I was back in shanghai
back where she
wants me to be
but it will be a day
a day maybe two
before I can return

yes
I will return to her
a day
a day, maybe two
me, locked
locked-in/locked-down
by a society
whose airlines
are all booked solid

booked solid
and full

arising feeling
arising feelings of love
and
what else can there be

arising feelings
arising feeling of settling down
and how can I

it is not like
we could just fall in love
and drive off to santa cruz
no
a price must be paid
the price of freedom
the price for her freedom
marriage
the price for her freedom
my freedom

arising feeling
arising feelings of love
and yes
I do love her
      but love
      it only leads
      to so many other things
      things that never seem to last

but I have to play this hand out
play this hand
as only a player like me can do
see you
my virtuous chinese love
see you in a day
a day, maybe two

23.

I guess
that I must call upon her
once more
I must see her a-new
see it first
for the second time

I must return
and gaze at her again

I do not know
what else I can do
except ride this train
to the logical limits
ride it
until it is no more

so tomorrow
I return
I will see her
for the first time
the second time

see her
the most beautiful woman
in shanghai
I must see her again
to know if I can
throw all that I am away
and place the flower pedals
at her feet
my heart it fills with anticipation

24.

I feel like
the bad boy of shanghai
the hotels do not want me
for I steal their local women
the people do not want me
my flesh is far too white
the government does not want me
just a piece or two of my
        american gold

I feel like
the bad boy of shanghai
well, how can I say it better
how can I say it more clearly
there is no finer way to put it
fuck them

for you see
I am american
brought up to believe
I am free
brought up to believe
I can do anything
and I can

so when push comes to shove
I'll do it all
and return like a king
to shanghai

they may not like me
they may not want the trouble I bring

they may say it
and I may agree
I am the bad boy of shanghai
      but bad is so good

25.

I want to see her again
see her for the first time
      the second time
I long to see her
question my judgment
test my vision
confirm
that she is
as beautiful as I believe

the perfection
and the perfect romance
a vision of a goddess seen
once more
seen again
the first time
      for the second time

26.

the bad boy is back
they remember me in shanghai
the hotel knows my look
the hotel knows my style
look out
the bad lad is back
and there is nothing that they can say
or do
my american express
        platinum card
my american dollars
speak louder than words

so if they don't like
don't like what they see
as far as I am concerned
they can go fuck themselves

shanghai
the bad boy is back

27.

there is a plastic smile
painted across the face
of my shanghai love
she met me at the airport
we have gone out to dine
there is a chinese lady singing
in bad english
she sings
poor soft pop

I would leave
but I am trapped
so all I can do
is stare out the window
into the rain
of this summer night
and watch the people pass
umbrellas in hand
and dream of other times
other places

28.

the lights are off
the night is late
as I hold her in my arms
no clothing between us
only first time kisses
first time love

her nervousness says, *No*
but I have never been one
to take, *No*
for an answer

in the complete darkness
there is only the feel
complimented
by the vague smells
odors
of our bodies
       this as our bodies merge

a touch
that will be known forever
how can it ever be forgotten
a touch
in the pitch black night
when all that can be known
is the touch
the first touch

29.

her odor was distant warm
like a summer night in shanghai
it was just that
a warm summer night in shanghai
and we were in love
I with her/her with I
and nothing else
really seemed to matter
not the self-imposed egotism
of the state secret police
who may at any moment
knock upon my door
not the desire
of the american dream
of the hotel deskman
awaiting downstairs
not her parents
who await
her non-existent return
nothing else could matter
for how could she ever return
after being touched
by the kiss of passion
touched by the kiss of the night
a kiss
I so dynamically delivered

the air was warm
she was warm
I was warm
the lights were out
the shades were drawn
leaving the night cold black

and I could feel her next to me
I could smell her gentle chinese skin
I could embrace her in many ways
there was nothing but the touch
our touch
her first touch
that
was
all
that
mattered

30.

if there was someone
I had to call
I would call them
and tell them
that I need them tonight
I need to be held
but there is no one
no one for me to call
the joke is
as it often is
on me
for on the other side
of the city
the other side of shanghai
there is a girl
who loves me all up
but no telephone
no eroticism permitted
in the china that is
so we make love in the day
and I take her home by taxi
in the night

in love/out of love
it is all the same
I have no one to call
and say that I need you tonight

31.

the smell of our love making
still permeates the air
as I lay here in bed
the bed which we made love upon
several times today

I can smell
our love in the air/on the sheets
and I can smell her scent
upon my skin
yes, I lay here alone
china has no room
for interracial love

so, as the night comes on
she, my love, goes her way
I go mine
and all that is left
is the scent
of the love we made today

32.

I look down and see
a head of long black hair
the head
lay upon my stomach
my dick
is softly/slowly being caressed
by an asian tongue
gently bitten
by chinese teeth

this could be heaven
but I look out
the twenty story window
but no
this is just shanghai

33.

if I were to believe
in the ways of destiny
I would have to believe
in her
if I were to believe
in forever
I would definitely believe
in love
but it seems
that I have
seen too much
too much
of what has gone down
too many one ways of no way
but I have to admit
that I have kept the dream

if I were to believe
in destiny
I would have to believe
in our love
for we met
in instant sight
and here we rest now

but everything comes and goes
I have to admit
it is sad
but every illusion
has its golden rainbow
just as every dreamer
has his day

so in the warm shanghai morning
I will wake
to her body next to mine
I almost wish
that it was forever
but forever
is always too short a time

but today
I will dream
that forever truly exists

34.

given the chance
would she be a mystic
she says, that many believe
she already is

given the chance
is such a mouth-full
for few
are ever born to see
    she obviously
    is a dreamer
she claims
to have prayed for me
    prayed for me
    to set her free
    free from the chains of china

perhaps it is I
who truly holds her key
I would be happy
to hand it over to her
    a key to the wind
    a key to the rain
    a key to all the dreams
    locked within her soul
    but the key
    it may cost me everything

the price for her freedom
    may be the price of my soul
    and to lose who I am
    so she can find
    who she wants to be
    anyone would have to question

35.

when the night's mission
is lost
lost and longing
I stare out across
a dark chinese city
alone

alone
I stand
alone
I am
I have no one fighting this fight
no one but me

a girl
she lay there
naked in form and function
naked to the touch
beauty the eyes
perfection for soul

she lay there
she sleep
lost in dreams
me, I stand here
stare out a window
across a broken city
dark/black

in my hands/in my grasp
I have her
her, the dream
her, the had

have and had
life and death
dreams and desires
and the mind of a fool
a fool
me
who believes
that there is actually
a possibility
that could make this last forever

forever…
when nothing ever lasts that long

36.

kiss for the first time
kiss from the first man
touch
touched deeply
love
the first time around

young/old
I do not know
it is all a state of mind
me, I walk the edge
kiss, softly kiss, sweetly
she has now become
the best kiss
I have ever known

it is almost sad
that our kisses will become stale
as kisses always do
the kisses will become old
before we can even
fully communicate

37.

maybe it's just
that we were together
long enough
but I leave
with a longing in my heart
a longing for her touch
a longing for her love
a longing to be held by her
once again

a fool
I am not
for a fool in love
I have been
but with every turn
there is another chance/another promise
of loving romance
but somehow
all of those
have led to nothing
nothing but longing
in the night

could it be
as poets have said
the answer is, in fact
love
all I know now
is that I feel the pain in my heart
a pain of remembrance
a pain of loss
and a desire to return to her love

38.

it is you
I am going back to see
your eyes
your hair
your naked body
next to mine
it is you
that I am returning for
no other reason
none even matters
your love
is all I seek
it is you
who I am returning for

39.

I take that long last look
out over the city of shanghai
the city
where I fell in love
but you know destiny
fucked me again
lied to me
cheated on me
the list
it never stops
but I guess
I should have known better
but you know
I always have been a fool
so, now all I can do
is let my heart hurt
for a little while
…it is good for the poetry
and then I will let it heal

I take my last look
out over the city of shanghai
as I ride up
in the glass elevator

fall in love
well, I had nothing better to do
but it would have been nice
if it felt good
for a little longer

40.

love
that I thought could never be
well somehow
I was right
another liar
in a player's night

I guess
I set the rules
playing as I do

I have to say
that I wish
it had turned out
another way

but once again
the joke
it is on me

so I sit here
nursing partial heart break
but I guess this feeling is better
than no feeling at all

I look out my hotel room window
into the shanghai sky
a few birds are flying
soon I will join them

hong kong
awaits my return

41.

her lies
were they so bad
the truth kills even more

ignorance is bliss
so it is said
I had to ask
I had to know
I pushed the limit
past its threshold
I questioned
why it was the way it was
the proof was in the pudding
I kept repeating to myself
and when the proof
didn't pan out
I asked
I should not have

*let's go back to the hotel*
the hotel where she now stayed with me
*let's go back to the hotel*
*I want to talk*
are the words that she spoke

inside
sitting between the two beds
the two beds
where we had made love
so many times
        ignorance was shattered
        pudding laid out
        plan and clear
        desires of the fool

        desired by a fool
        tears flowing
        she had been ravished
        lost innocence
                ungainable
                unreturnable

it is only there once
grabbed by the hands
of the demon
taken from me
long before
I could changed formed destinies

and the demon's path
who can see it

the ways of the world
who can change them

once destiny had laid down
who can/who will

I believe we all would/could
if we were only given the chance

so, I had lost
she had lost
gaining
was only the desire of a fool

change it
I will try

but to the untamed sorcery
of the world
what can a blind man do

ignorance is bliss
so it is said
      silent listening
      faithful trusting
      no questions asked
      none answered

so should be the rule
to a life with no pain

42.

perhaps something is lost
perhaps something is gained
      I no longer know
perhaps I no longer care

maybe I am too sensitive
but I wish it all had been different

I sit here
five star restaurant
I sleep in a
five star hotel
I am surrounded
by a minus three star world
and there seems no longer
any way out

bottled water
I drink it down
bottled time
can I hold it/remove it
if only I could change it

but there is no longer
a horizon
I watched its
orange and red colors
fade to the black
last evening in flight

no where left to go
nothing left to feel

for it all adds up to
is the same disappointment
and pain

but if only it were different
if only
every dream
could be held/could be lived
but they all seem to be robbed
> by the vice grip
> of this world
> by the fools
> and their desires
> by the gods
> who do not care
> by a life
> that is unforgiving
> and by time
> that never slows down

so hit me up
with another cappuccino
cappuccino
if you please
a bite or two
of the lobster salad
that I do not even want
and then
I will be back on the street(s)

43.

am I suppose
to simply forget
can it be expected
that it is so easy
am I to have
no feelings
like a yogi
or a rock

I care
I want my life to be different
I want her life to be different
I want us to meet as we did
and live in a field
of newly bloomed flowers
forever

but the world
in all its desires
has taken that from us
     taken it from me/taken it from her
and left us
tired and used
like an old weathered
walked on
dirt road
which no longer
can serve any purpose
but to separate
the strands of grass
until time
eventually reclaims
all that it owns

44.

dining alone
it has become difficult
no longer are
the chinese eyes that loved me
gazing into mine
from across the table
      I am lost
      both the love
      and the desire
      for love
      have been ripped from me

the evening falls
on this asian city
the waitress
brings around
pre-lighted candles
in prefabricated candle stands
covered with
yellowing glass

she places a candle
on my table
and a few minutes later returns
and with no expression of remorse
removes it
to be strategically placed
at another table

the world
is now a thousand times darker
and I have to hold back the tears

45.

I walk out
onto the streets
the heat is intense
and I am fucked up
    looking for a reason why
    looking for a reason to forget
    looking for illusion
    …any illusion will do
but I walk out
onto the streets
alone
after making love to a bar stool
after making love to a  b a r  m a i d
not so beautiful but she obviously
loves my tips

but, I am sorry
it is simply not enough
I cannot go back
go back
and be the way I was
pretend
when there is
no pretending left
simply put
I am different
    different from then
    different from the man
    even different from my friends
I can never go back

46.

the streets of hong kong
are hot
too very hot
and I am in too deep
I wish
I knew
a way out
but there seems to be none
so I wallow
in it
of it
for it
        love touched
        love felt
        but a love
        taken from me
        by the demon
        of life

I could return to her arms
I want to return
I need to return
to touch her
to love her
to make love with her
but I have nothing to offer her
        what she desires of me
          no, I cannot marry her
                the most beautiful woman
                in shanghai
so I sit here
lost in confusion
lost in the desire of hong kong

seeking a method
to return to her
seeking a reason
to return to california
but there is nothing
there seems to be none
so, all I can do
       on this night
       this hot night
       is to walk the streets
       go to a bar
       and drink
       all the feelings
       of emptiness away
       drink
       like so many have done
       before me

       a fool's escape
       in a fool's world

47.

black hairs
long and asian
they mix with mine
in my brush
      a reminder
      of what once was
      a reminder
      of our time together
I think
that I must cry
a tear or two

48.

I walk outside
the heat hits me
like a passionate wave
of silence
I have developed a taste for it
I have prepared
now I sit/I wait
to move northward again
into the mouth of the dragon
into the midst of its flame
      northward
      again

it is hot there too
hot as well
hotter in many ways
than it is here
but there lies
the cool breath of passion
the lips
to be placed upon mine
      cool and hot
      disparity
      the way of life

so, now I wait
surrounded by walls
I could be outside
where the women are
full of style/full of beauty
but I have become so tired
of the chase
so I sit
so I wait

surrounded by the walls
of this first class lounge

I am alone
alone
except for the lounge attendant
who is not much to look at

I am obviously
an annoyance to her
      her privacy
      her solitude
      her getting paid
      for doing nothing

but then
every something
is an obvious nothing
giving birth
to the realm of reason
the realm of compassion
the realm of passion
me, I am heading for it
on my way very soon
so that order may be restored
      restored to the city of heat
      restored to a lounge attendant's aloneness
      restored into the arms of cooling love
      cooling passion
      into the fire of a dragon a flame
      that is too hot

49.

I eat chinese potato chips
I drink chinese coffee
as I read the words of
marguerite duras
so eloquent
that they bring tears
to my eyes

the world spins
at thirty thousand feet
in my first class section

me, I long once again
for something else
but in that longing
I am more than content
        content in the someday
        content in the love
        content in all the discontentment
        I read on
        I drink on
        I eat on

50.

it was raining in L.A.
as I drove down the street
a woman sitting next to me
another one on my mind

who was to say
who could have seen
one love coming
another one going
and it took six months
for it to happen
        six months
        maybe more

but in every dream
there is a desire
in every desire
there is a dream
        a cast to the shadows
        of life's perfection

I have here
now in front of me
what I longed for
        six months before
        maybe more

51.

she lays there
in all here splendor and glory
a goddess in her own right
asleep to the physical world

her black hair merges
into the reflection of the night
her skin
into the soft whiteness
of the sheets
upon which she lay

and yes, I love her
love her like no other
love her like no one before
and I can not help but wonder
I cannot help but imagine
where her dreams are taking her
where it is they go
for it was not long ago
that it was they
that brought me to her

52.

I stepped unknowingly
into the dream of illusion
somewhere out there
in the old temple
by the sea

I stepped in the door of illusion
I never saw it coming
I never saw when it came

and once inside
it was all given to me
and instantly
it was all taken away

illusion...

53.

wordy discourse
about our love
in a language
I do not understand

words are spoken
treaties made
and it is all about me
but it all passes me by

there she sits
in her valley girl glasses
stunning underneath them
    as the reflections
       of fluorescent lights glow

there she sits
in all her radiance
knowing the moves
discussing them all
laying the foundation
of our love/for our love
and I do not have any idea
what is going on

and it is said
that there is no imperfection
only perfection
always a reason why
but I think
this is a lie

yet, there she sits

in a dress
which is worn by many
but she is so much higher
so much more
than all of them

maybe it is a sign of tradition
maybe a sign of the times
but when all is lost
no longer do I believe
that something can be gained

life/love/loss
it is simply the desire
laid down by the demons
lived by fools
who linger
in this shanghai night

*forever...*
I hear the word spoken
spoken in chinese

family discussions
and decisions are made
me, I have no idea
what the fuck is being said

but the sounds linger
in both of my ears
in the volume
of a shanghai night

me, I know
all that is being said
can add up to nothing
all the proposed proposals
all the parental consent
really means not a thing
yes, I know
the debate is on
but when all is said and all is done
nothing will not equal something
for the only path I can take
now that my vestal virgin dream
has been robed
is out

that is the way out
I see it
over there

54.

kisses longed for
kisses lived
promises made
promises denied
and we all
are bound
by the cruel
hands of fate

55.

I lay in her arms
I lay in them at this moment
she watches me write
in a language
that she cannot understand
I lay in her arms
and I think
of the first kiss
that she gave me
I lay in her arms
and I think
of the first love
that we made
I lay in her arms
I hold on to her love
and I hate
the city of shanghai
I hate the demons
that live within its bounds
I hate the destiny of god and mind
and I hate the fact
that a man of little consequence
was allowed to drive himself
into the realms of her body
and force himself upon her
before she and I could ever met

and if this were any other daydream
if it were any other song
I would turn it off
do something/do anything
that would allow me
to make it all change

but this world is full of fools
and if I believed in heaven
I would certainly
wish them all to go to hell
but this is china
no religion
only the state
and where do the wicked
do their time

so I am robbed of my fantasy
as she was robbed of her chance
and in any other world
there would be retribution
but it seems in this one
that there will be none

56.

I kiss her one time
I kiss her five times
as she softly sleeps
      a vision of the goddess
      I have woke
      to find laying nude
      in all of her glory
      all of her elegance
is there anything more to life
once, perhaps
I thought that there was
now I know
there is nothing
nothing more than this
quiet passion
laying there asleep
lost deeply in a dream of love
      I kiss her
      softly
      one more time
      than I return
      to lay with her
      asleep

57.

it is almost amazing
how long time convictions
are lost
and surrendered
in moments of passion
in moments of desire

it is almost unbelievable
how long time knowledge
long time dreams
are cast
to the realms
of forgotten fantasies
when lips are embraced
by a love
that could have been forever
but was only for a moment
in desired time

58.

and I hope to see you again
in the cool air of winter
when there is angels
in your eyes
and angels
on your pillow
and the soft gentle wind
touches your chinese skin

remember me

59.

there are no stars in shanghai
not a one
light up the sky
there is no moon in shanghai
only the dim reflection
of the yellow city lights
which shine
in the gray blue haze

and if this were
any other time
or if the past
did not hold us bound
I would live here forever
live here with her
and let each day
slowly pass
into our embrace

60.

I want to fall down and cry
I want to forget
I want to be given the reason
for my no reason
I want to know why
in the kiss of oblivion
in the kiss of death
in the kiss of love ever-after
in the kiss of forgiveness
in the kiss of the moment
when there is nothing in the moment
by the promise of love

torn between the world and reason
a tear in her eye
brings a tear to mine
I throw down the paper
I no longer care for the words
I throw down everything
I want to die
I want to cry
or I want
a reason why

61.

love
it sits next to me
love
but not mine

yes
I was a believer
      holding hands
      making promises
      promises in the night
      a night that will last forever
      but promises
      it seems that they never last
           making promises
              one can never keep

love
I have been here/there before
      wrapped
      in its embrace
      wrapped
      in its entanglement
      its fragrance
      it is so sweet

I am reminded
of a childhood time
a summer's day
a church outing
when we had ridden in a car
far-far away
we had seen the sights
a friend and I

came back upon the car
and there was the grandmother
who had come along for the ride
praying to god
praying out loud
to please take her home
I wished then
as I wish now
that I had a home
I wish then
as I wish now
that prayers were answered

      I remember the dream
      of the love
      of the love
      I had just today
      in shanghai

      I remember the communion
      the prayers
      for it all
      to have been different
      for it all
      to have turned out differently

      I remember my psychic attempts
      to change the past
      but I could not cross
      the boundaries of time

I am reminded
yes, I cannot help but think
of those things

but, I was still torn away from her
torn away by something
which I could not control
torn away by my desires
torn away by the desires
of the world
torn away by the desires of demons
I was torn away none-the-less

but now I am here
here in a restaurant
lovers they sits next to me
the two of them
to my right
        holding hands
        promising
        kissing
me
I am alone
it seems to always
end up that way
me
I am more than fucked up
and the wine continues
        hiding me
        blocking me
        protecting me
        shading my field of vision
        keeping the tears

      from coming
      to my eyes

love
it sits next to me
and I am reminded
of other times

62.

some how
I beat the rain home
I do not know how
I look out my
eighteenth story window
the streets are wet
and the rain
it is falling down
me, well I…
I will fall asleep
my head
it is a-spinning
no-love
no-one
I want to…
I want to know why
but there is no answers
I do not want
to be alone
but there is no one

      spinning reason(s) in a poets words
      I try
      I try
      I must try harder
      to forget
      forget
      forget it all
      forget everyone
      as I cry
      my drunken self to sleep

alone
the rain

it is raining
I hear it coming down
      clean me
      cleanse me please
      I do not want
      to have to forever cry

63.

it rains
as I fly out of hong kong
fly away
away from my love in china
      away from the demons
      away from the goddess
      away from a land
      too far lost
      thus too far gone

it rains as I fly out of hong kong
have I been on this island
concealed from the mainland
too long or maybe too short a time
I do not know

it rains as I fly out of hong kong
I see the raindrops
on the window of the plane
I see their imprint
on the waters of the bay
      the dark dirty green
      water of the harbor
      connected to the ocean
            the place of freedom
            the place of birth
            a place of life

it rains as I fly out of hong kong
a dream away
I dream into the night
I dream of the kisses
I have left behind
of the love I have known

too soon
too long
who can ever be sure
the rain
kisses from goddess
kisses from heaven
a remembrance of the freedom
       I have known
of the freedom
       I have felt
of the freedom
       never seen
              for a century or so
there on the mainland
hong kong
       connected to the mainland
       the mainland of china
china
where my love awaits my non-existent return
she does not know
that she will never see me again

my love
she will never see me again my love

for her I cry a tear
for myself I cry a tear
a tear in the rain
       it will never be seen
       it will never be known

rain, a kiss form god
rain, a kiss from the heavens

give my china love
a kiss for me Mr. Rain


it rains as I fly out of hong kong
a land
leased to freedom
       connected to a land living in fear
       kiss them both goodbye for me mr. rain
kiss them for me

it rains as I fly
out of hong kong

64.

night lost
lost to day
dreams devoured
in the lies of life

time lost
time torn
there is never
a tomorrow
only the lie
that awaits
on the horizon

65.

it is the story of life
balloons blowing away in the wind
merging with the sky
they just slip away
and then they are gone

and no
it is not right
no
I do not believe it is right
but I guess
no one ever said
that life was right

yet the philosophers
try to find
the reasons

the mystics
say that there are none
        but another word spoken
        is another lie told
        and all it is to me
        is simply not right

it is the story of my life
the beautiful balloons that slip from my hand
and blow away
        into the wind
        into the sky
                goodbye

66.

some how I think all I want to do
is to go back to shanghai
where I lived
in the best hotel
ate the best food
the city had to offer
and made love
to the most beautiful woman
in shanghai

memories die hard
when there is nothing
to replace them with

and when life offers nothing
but further complications
all that is sought
is a way out

somewhere on that road
life on the hard road
I lost all my dreams

some how
each time I return home
they shatter further
before my eyes
leaving me empty
and longing

where there is everything
nothing has little to offer

and when there are no hugs
no stolen kisses
and no love made
what is left
only alone

I think I want to return to shanghai
where the most beautiful woman
of the city awaits
where my plastic money
pays the bills
and where everyday offers
the freedom
of nothing having to be done
    no complications
      simply making love
      with in the walls
      of the best hotel in shanghai

I long to return

67.

I need to call you
and say good night
say I love you
but you are a million miles away
in shanghai

and if I had the chance
tonight
I would hold you in my arms
and
I would be in love with you
      in love with you
         all over again

but all I can do
is dream of calling you
for telephones have not reached
the  common man's home
      the average home
      in the average city
      in the land of the people
      the people's republic of china

I received your letter
in my Post Office Box today
but written words
do not equal spoken words
and spoken words
do not equal love

      you wrote
      that you loved me
      yes, I know

and if I could go to you tonight
you know that I would
      but I am here
           with all my reasons
           you are there
           held by the bars
           of the bamboo curtain
all I can do
is dream of you
and know that there is
nothing left for me here
    no woman
    no love
    no one to call
    no friends worth having
    not even a family
    just myself
        lost in love
        with no love
        a kiss of death
        a kiss good night

I would go there
and stay with you forever
if only I knew how

        it has been
        three weeks
        maybe four
        since I last saw you
        last told you
        that I love you

yes, I love you
my incomplete desire of a dream
I  l o v e  y o u   but I am here
      alone
      tonight
      wishing that I could call you
      and say
      good night, I love you

but
there is no way
I can telephone you
so, I will go to sleep tonight
      to sleep early
      let no man
      no time
      no reason
      no lie
      be my master

to sleep early tonight
and I will say to you
as I am slowly falling asleep
good night
I love you

68.

I look at the photographs
that I took of her
the perfect woman
on the first day
that our eyes met

I look at the photographs
they are some what blurred
some what distant
some how not clear

unclear
like the memory
of the feeling
that I had
when I first saw her
      the perfect woman
      the most beautiful woman in shanghai

I look at the photographs
the colors they fade
into the burning night fog
a fog
like which
hangs over the city of shanghai
brought about by the industrialization
      brought about by the modernization
      brought about by desire

  desire
that gave her to me
desire
that took her from me

desire
the destroyer
and the creator
of the world

I look at the photographs
that I took of her on the first night
the first night
that we were together
        together
                lost in love
                lost in desire
                dreaming of a chance
                fantasizing of a dream

those photographs are not clear unclear
        like what has become of our dream
        like what has become of our love
        like what has become of our chance


the colors they fade
into the haze
the same haze that is formed
over the skies of shanghai

69.

the ocean waves roar outside
it is so close to me
so close to her
she lives in shanghai
city by the sea

she lives by the pacific ocean
I live by the pacific ocean

yet we are thousands of miles apart
millions of lives apart
      so close
      yet so far

perhaps someday
she will touch the ocean
at the same time
that I touch the ocean
and we will be as the raindrops
falling down from the sky
being singular as they fall
than entering the whole
becoming one
      one with in the totality
      her and I
      again together
      as one
            forever

70.

shanghai
whispers in my ear
reminding me of the love
that I once had
reminding me of the love
which I once felt
the tease of the goddess

shanghai
whispers in my ear
asking me
why I have not returned
asking me
will I return soon
a tear
touches my ear

shanghai
whispers in my ear
I tell her
to read my letter
telling her why
I cannot be with her

she tells me
that she will wait for me forever

shanghai
whispers in my ear
it makes me want to cry

71.

she calls me on the telephone
from a million miles away
        she calls
            the connection is bad
I can barely hear her words
she asks me
        when I will return to her
            to hold her once again
but how can I ever go back there
and lose myself again
in the fields of illusion

now/this it is not unlike my poetry
once it was very vague
symbols in the written word
now
I more or less
just tell my story
speak it straight and clear

and it is not unlike my art
once abstract
a movement in color
now it has
slowly taken form

perhaps it is all like my life
        like the spirituality
           that it revolves around

perhaps, it too
my life
was hazy

it now has become more clear
how could I ever go back
to that intensity
that was known
while I was held in her arms
how can I ever go back g o
back to that insanity
that was brought on
by our love

on the telephone
the word are hard to hear

I hear her whisper
in the distance
she will phone again
I hear her say
in the haze
that she will call me again
from the international telephone station

time
perhaps that will give me time
time
to think of an answer
that I may give to her
an answer that says
if I had the money
I would go and live the dream
if I had the ticket
I would return for the illusion
but not the lie

to hide from all that haunts me here
to hide from all that I am not
but I know I must tell her
I can never return
to that kiss of insanity
that brush with death in the heat
of the shanghai summer nigh

72.

it remains
in itself
of itself
in a painting
that hangs over my bed
        a painting of freedom
        a painting of love
        a painting of the moment
        I call it
        the flowers of shanghai

it is not that it was so long ago
or even that it was so far away
but in the caress
of the distress
a moment of love
was lost forever
and if I could ever go back
you know that
I probably would

I would walk in the wisdom
walk in the heated summer rain
and be in love again
the flowers of shanghai

73.

I saw a movie about china yesterday
it brought tears to my eyes
I sat there in the dark crying
for what I had come to know there
crying
for what I had come to lose there
china
it has not been like that with any place
before
not
india
Thailand
korea
japan
        the loves had/the loves lost

no
I can think of these places
think as I will
see them in memories
on the screen before me
but the vision
does not bring tears to my eyes
china
it is different

I saw a movie about china yesterday
it brought tears to my eyes
        it brought thoughta
        memories
        to my mind
        china

      in the evening last
      I went to the house
      of a woman who loves me
           chinese in origin
           but  anything
           but chinese of mind

I went there
to love her
for I knew I could find physical love
in her form
      embraced/touched
and as I lay there making love with her
it brought tears to my mind

tears for china
tears for what I had
tears for what I had come to know

I saw a movie of china yesterday
it brought tears to my eyes

74.

had I stayed there
holding her
or brought her here
across the sea
it would have been
old by now
and regrets
there would have been many

the moment(s) of love
        they were embraced
        she held me so tight
but that was nine months ago
it seems like many years
        it feels like
        forever ago

and had I loved her
here in america
than all the volumes
filled with all the further illusion(s)
would have been cut short
        so forever
        and love
        and all that can
        and can never be
        who makes the choice
                what is the best choice
                volumes of new poetry
                written about
                meaningful/meaningless
        or a love
        that never dies?

www.ingramcontent.com/pod-product-compliance
Lightning Source LLC
Chambersburg PA
CBHW072158100426
42738CB00011BA/2467